Florence & Pisa Travel Guide

Attractions, Eating, Drinking, Shopping & Places To Stay

Ryan Wilson

Copyright © 2014, Astute Press
All Rights Reserved.

No part of this publication may be reproduced, stored in a retrieval system, or transmitted, in any form or by any means without the prior written permission of the publisher, nor be otherwise circulated in any form of binding or cover other than that in which it is published and without similar condition being imposed on the subsequent purchaser.

If there are any errors or omissions in copyright acknowledgements the publisher will be pleased to insert the appropriate acknowledgement in any subsequent printing of this publication.

Although we have taken all reasonable care in researching this book we make no warranty about the accuracy or completeness of its content and disclaim all liability arising from its use

Table of Contents

Florence 6
   Culture..8
   Location & Orientation 9
   Climate & When to Visit...9

Sightseeing Highlights..11
   Accademia Gallery 11
   Il Duomo & Campanile Bell Tower 13
   Ponte Vecchio 16
   Uffizi Gallery 18
   Piazza della Signoria 19
   Castello del Trebbio 21
   The Medici Villas 22
   Piazzale Michelangelo 23
   Boboli Garden & Pitti Palace 24
   Basilica di San Miniato al Monte 26

Recommendations for the Budget Traveller 27
   Places to Stay 27
   Hotel Sampaoli..28
      Garibaldi's Relais & Charme 29
      Hostel Greci 30
      David Inn 30
      Soggiorno Pitti..31
   Places to Eat 32
      Le Campane 32
      IL GIOVA...33
      Il Pizza Iuolo 34
      Grom 35
      Blue River...35
   Places to Shop...36
      Stockhouse Il Giglio 37
      Farmacia del Mercato Centrale.....................................37
      Monaco Metropolitano 38

Pisa 40
   Culture..42
   Location & Orientation...42

Climate & When to Visit 43

Sightseeing Highlights 44
Piazza dei Miracoli (Square of Miracles) 44
Leaning Tower of Pisa 46
Bell Tower of San Nicola Church 50
Duomo di Pisa (Cathedral of Pisa) 52
Battistero (Baptistery) 54
Camposanto (Walled Cemetery) 56
Museo dell'Opera del Duomo 57
Museo Nazionale di San Matteo 59
Palazzo dell' Orologio 60
Campanile di San Nicola (St. Nicolas Belfry) 62
Museum of the Ancient Ships 63
Ussero Café 64

Recommendations for the Budget Traveller 66
Places to Stay 66
Hotel Granduca Tuscany 66
Hotel Capitol 67
Hotel la Torre 68
Hotel Francesco 68
Eden Park Tuscany Resort 69
Places to Eat & Drink 69
Il Montino 69
Ristorante Turrido 70
Peperosa Pisa 70
L'Ostellino 71
Coccio Bar & Gelateria 71
Places to Shop 72
Corso Italia 72
Borgo Stretto 73
Piazza dei Cavalieri & Ponti di Mezzo 73
Piazza delle Vettovaglie 74
Via Buonarroti & Via San Martino 74

Florence

Florence (Firenze) is Tuscany's capital and was once Italy's capital. The city is known for its importance during the Renaissance between the 14th and 17th centuries. Today Florence offers stunning artwork, galleries, manicured gardens, winding streets and delightful waterfront shops.

The Renaissance (meaning 'rebirth' in French) was a cultural movement which spread across Europe and resulted in the rebirth of education, teaching and learning in its many forms.

As one of the most visited cities in Europe during the past 1000 years, Florence charms its way into the visitor's heart like no other.

In sciences, Leonardo da Vinci spearheaded the study of the human anatomy, while Galileo revealed that the Earth revolved around the Sun. In politics ancient texts untouched for over 1000 years were uncovered and debated, while most notably, the arts took a new life form of their own.

Fundamental new techniques were imposed, and artists learned how to paint and sketch in three dimensions, bringing more life, drama and emotion to their works. In architecture, buildings were bigger and grander than ever, taking into account new rules on proportion and taking inspiration from the classical past. All of this in turn influenced painting, sculpture and architecture of the highest calibre.

Although modern day Florence may be a little different, its greatest attraction is the fact that these inspiring paintings, faultless sculptures and seamless architecture still remain today. Away from the city, some of Tuscany's finest gardens, villas and vistas can be experienced, while taking in one of the world's greatest city sunsets.

Culture

As grand churches and basilicas sprung up during the medieval times, followed by the splendor of the Renaissance, the trend of Florence's aesthetically pleasing culture continues today through some of the world's leading designers like Gucci and Ferragamo. Florence has had style for over 1000 years, and the trendy locals show no sign of changing that any time soon. Stylish boutiques line the city's streets whilst the masterpieces of the past reflect in their windows, while Florentines themselves tend to make an effort when it comes to dressing, especially for formal occasions and dinners, and the dress sense of the locals can be seen on the streets any time of day.

It is not just the appearance that Italians like to keep in check. Most Italians will only drink the odd one or two glasses wine or beer with an evening meal, and excessive drinking – especially over dinner – is rare and highly frowned upon. Like in many parts of Italy, Florentines greet each other with a light embrace and a kiss on each cheek, and it is not uncommon for men to do this when greeting each other.

Florence's culture is however most famous for its artistic heritage. Cimabue and Giotti, the fathers of Italian painting; Donatello, Masacchio, Botticelli, Da Vinci and Michelangelo all lived and worked in Florence, and all contributed to the city's stunning art.

Location & Orientation

Located 129 kilometres (80 miles) from Italy's west coast and the Mediterranean, and 230 kilometres (145 miles) northwest of the capital Rome, Florence's spot on the boot of Italy lies in the heart of Tuscany, the country's most famous region, along the River Arno. Surrounded by a circle of sandstone hills and the Apennine Mountain Range a little further out, Florence is located perfectly for ease of access, and for exploring the nearby cities and regions.

The city itself is divided into numerous neighbourhoods – or areas – which are all jammed close together. Duomo, Piazza del Signoria, San Lorenzo, Piazza Santa Trinita, Santa Maria Novella, San Marco, Santa Croce, Oltrarno make up the different parts of the city, with many of them being createdfor the family rivalries during the Renaissance.

Climate & When to Visit

With its Mediterranean climate, the city can get hot during the summer months of July and August, with temperatures in the late 30's (°C) not uncommon. July and August are also peak tourist season, as well as vacation time in Italy, meaning just like many parts of the country it is not uncommon to find local shops and businesses closed for a few weeks.

The brief winter In Florence is mild, and can be quite pleasant and crisp, with a few rainy days scheduled each month between November and April. Temperatures do get down to around 1°C (33°F). With the summer months of July and August averaging highs of 30°C (87 °F), the best time of year to visit is during the city's pleasant autumn months of September and October. There is still plenty of sunshine to be had at this time year, however temperatures are a little lower, and more comfortable, and the city is a lot less crowded. Spring (March-May) is also a great time to visit, although there is typically a little more rainfall this time of year in comparison to the autumn.

For up to date weather forecasts for Florence, see:
http://www.theweathernetwork.com/weather/itxx0028

Sightseeing Highlights

Accademia Gallery

Originally a 14th century hospital, the Accademia Gallery opened up as Europe's first Academy of Drawing in 1563, and is still in operation today. Many of Florence's most renowned artists including Giorgio Vasari attended the academy to increase its prestige, and today it is visited by millions of tourists every year. With numerous works including Botticelli's world famous Madonna and Child and Madonna of the Sea, and Giambologna's original plaster copy of the Rape of the Sabines, as well as works by Filippino Lippi, Pontormo, and Bronzino.

While many tourists would happily line up to see the aforementioned works, it is one striking piece of art which makes the Accedemia Gallery the number one place in Florence to visit. After spending almost 400 years outside, Michelangelo's David was moved to the Accademia Gallery in 1873. Sculpted between 1501 and 1504 by a then 26 year old Michelangelo, David is a true masterpiece and confirmed his creator as the most celebrated sculptor of his day.

The statue was originally said to be part of a collection of 12 proposed sculptures from the Old Testament, which were to be placed on the buttresses of the Cathedral of Santa Maria del Fiore. Two of these sculptures had already been completed, Donatello's Joshua, and Agostino'sHercules, both made of Terracotta, and it was actually Agostino who began the original work of David, however he only got as far as roughly shaping the legs before his association with the work was ended for reasons unknown. After 25 years of neglect, the contract was eventually offered to Michelangelo, who began working on the sculpture within a week.

There are many stories and tales of how Michelangelo spent his days planning and executing the transition of a 16ft block of marble into one of the world's most remarkable pieces of art, including how he spent eight hours each day 'staring' at the block for four months, before eventually using his hands. While many stories remain unaccounted for, what is still clear to this day is the masterpiece that this block of marble has become.

With proportions and features clearly indicating that it was designed to be looked at from below, the statue's sheer, imposing size comes as a surprise to many visitors. David was originally placed high on a pedestal outside the Piazza della Signora, which now houses a replica. From here his eyes were said to be gazing towards his opponent Goliath, with his anxious emotion masterfully recreated with the tendons in his neck standing out, his tight upper lip the veins in his lowered right hand bulging out.

While photographs are not allowed, the statue of David is memorable to see in real life, and should top most Florence itineraries regardless of your fondness for art.

Via Ricasoli, 66
50122 Florence, Italy
Tel.: 055 215449
Web: www.accademia.firenze.it/new/ (Italian)
Web: www.florence-museum.com/Accademia

Entrance: €15.25
Opening hours: Tuesday to Sunday: 8:15am to 6:50pm.

Il Duomo & Campanile Bell Tower

One of the most iconic images of Renaissance architecture, Il Duomo and Campanile Bell Tower stand next to each other overlooking the Piazza del Signora, and both offer breathtaking views of the city's terracotta rooftops from their respective lookout points.

The duomo, also known as Basilica Di Sant Maria Del Fiore, has long been the regarded as the heart of the city, both geographically and religiously, and has remained one of the symbolic images of Florence's skyline for over 600 years. Almost 175 years in the making, construction began in September 1296 under the direction of Arnolfo di Cambio, with famous names such as Giotto and Brunelleschi playing a significant role in the design later on. It was officially completed in 1469 when a copper ball crafted by local Florentine sculptor Andrea del Verrocchio was placed at the top of the cathedral's Dome.

For a rewarding 360° panoramic view of the city, a climb of 463 steps is necessary to reach the domes lookout point. From here, a breathtaking view of Florence surrounded by the Tuscan hills can be enjoyed.

While the cathedrals exterior is as breathtaking as any Renaissance building, the huge interior can take a little exploring to unveil the treasures that it holds, due to an empty impression given by many of the rooms and halls. Many of the cathedrals original decorations have been lost over the years, or transferred to the Museum Opera del Duomo.

One of the most breathtaking adornments within the cathedral is on the dome ceiling itself. Giorgio Vasari's fresco of the Last Judgement, which he began in 1572, took seven years to complete. Vasari died before the completion of the work, which was taken over by Federico Zuccari and a number of other collaborators. The crypt of Santa Reparata – the original fifth century church that once stood on the present site -is housed within the cathedral and contains ruins of the church, as well as some Roman remains of the streets that it was built upon.

The Campanile - also known as Giotto's Bell Tower or Campanile di Giotto, was named after its original designer Giotto di Bondone, and stands adjacent to Il Duomo. Built as a bell tower for the cathedral, work began on the Campanile 40 years after construction had begun on Il Duomo, although the tower was completed 110 years before the cathedrals official completion date. At a height of the 84m (276-ft), the tower was primarily worked on by Giotto until his death in 1337, with only the lower floor completed at this stage. Giotto's successor - Andrea Pisano - diagnosed that the original plans meant the tower had a high risk of collapsing, and went on to doubled the thickness of the tower walls, as well as adding the statues to the tower's exterior. The top three levels were completed by Francesco Talenti, who added numerous windows to atone for the base's perceived density.

The Campanile also offers one of the best lookout points in the city, with a climb of 414 steps required to reach the top. From here one can take an alternative look across the city, with a close up exterior view of the duomo's dome.

Piazza Duomo,
Firenze, 50122
Italy
Tel.: (+39) 055 215380
Web: www.duomofirenze.it
Email: info@duomofirenze.it

Admission to the cathedral is free, while there is an €8 charge to visit the dome and crypt.
Opening hours: Monday, Wednesday and Friday, 10:00am until 5:00pm; Thursday, 10:00am until 3:30pm; Saturday, 10:00am until 4:45pm; Sunday, 1:30pm until 4:45pm.

Ponte Vecchio

Meaning 'Old Bridge' in English, the Ponte Vecchio is the oldest of Florence's bridges and today remains one of the most symbolic images of the city. The bridge was originally thought to have been built long before the Renaissance period, with it first appearing in a document in 996, before being badly damaged by severe flooding in 1117.

The bridge was finally rebuilt in 1333 only to be destroyed again the same year, and it wasn't until 1345 when it was completed to its current state as part of the wave of Renaissance construction. The Ponte Vecchio was the only bridge in Florence to survive the attacks during the Second World War, which was said to be an express order by Hitler, who supposedly believed the bridge was too beautiful to blow up.

The bridge is well known for the shops that are stacked along and hang over the edge of the bridge. The shops on the bridge were originally used as workshops, and were also rented by butchers and tanners. In 1593 they were replaced by goldsmiths due to the sheer amount of waste and foul smell caused by the current occupants. Today the premises are favoured by jewelers as well as shoemakers and tourist shops.

One of the most interesting attractions for tourists visiting the Ponte Vecchio and the nearby PlazzadellaSignoria, is the Vasari corridor. Almost a kilometre in length, Giorgio Vasari created the elevated, covered walkway under the instruction of Grand Duke Cosimo I de' Medici in 1564, who wanted to move freely and conveniently between his residence at the Palazzo Pitti on the north side of the Arno River, to the Palazzo Vecchio and the government palace. The walkway begins at the Palazzo Vecchio and joins the Uffizi gallery, before crossing the Ponte Vecchio above the shops. When crossing the bridge, there are numerous panoramic windows looking out onto the River Arno. Whist the walkway is a unique attraction; numerous parts are closed to visitors.

Ponte Vecchio,
50125 Firenze,
Italy
Tel.: (+39) 055 290 832

Uffizi Gallery

One of the oldest museums in the western world, the Uffizi - which means 'offices' – was originally built as offices for the Florentine magistrates, and is now one of the most visited museums in the world. The gallery is housed in the building designed by Vasari in 1560, and built by Cosimo I of Medici. The collection began in 1574 by Cosimo's son, Francesco I, who converted the second floor into a place where he was said to have wanted 'to walk in with paintings, sculptures and other precious things'.

The sheer collection housed at the Uffizi – said to be only masterpieces – is regarded by many as incomparable to any other collection in the world, and features a plethora of works from some of the world's most renowned artists, including Leonardo da Vinci, Sandro Botticelli, Giotto, Michelangelo, Raphael, Cimabue and many more.

Via della Ninna, 5,
50122 Firenze, Italy
Tel.: (+39) 055 238 8651
Web: www.uffizi.firenze.it

Admission is €8.50, cash only.
Opening hours: Tuesday to Sunday, 8:15am until 6:50pm.

Piazza della Signoria

Adorned with 16th century statues, fountains, and classic Renaissance architecture, The Piazza della Signoria has remained the center of political life in the city for almost 700 years, and is dominated by the striking Palazzo Vecchio which overlooks the L shaped plaza. It was here were many spectacles of great triumph were seen, such as the much celebrated return of the Medici in 1530. Today the square is still seen as the ideal meeting place for local Florentines and tourists alike, due to its ideal location close to the Ponte Vecchio bridge and Arno River, the Duomo, and the Uffizi.

The many sculptures in Piazza della Signoria are associated with past political undertones, including Michelangelo's David, which has since been moved to the Galleria dell'Accademia and replaced with a replica. Originally standing tall outside the Palazzo Vecchio, David was seen as an indication of Florence's bold opposition of the later, more ruthless Medici, while Bandinelli's Hercules and Cacus, now standing to the right of David's replica, was appointed by the Medici to display their physical power after their return from displacement.

The building on the corner of the square is the Loggia dei Lanzi, also known as the Loggia della Signoria, and is effectively an open-air sculpture gallery of Renaissance art. Featuring three huge arches which are open to the rest of the square, the building features Cellini's 1554 statue of Perseo holding the head of Medusa, which took ten years in the making and was seen as a blunt reminder of the consequences of opposing the Medici. Giambologna's Rape of the Sabines, is also featured amongst many other beautiful sculptures found beneath the arches of the Loggia dei Lanzi.

Many tourists can spend a long afternoon here people watching while enjoying an Italian latte or an offering from one of the nearby gelato stores, and there are also numerous restaurants around the square with great outdoor dining areas, for breakfast, lunch, or a formal dinner.

Piazza della Signoria, 5,
50122 Firenze
Web: www.piazza-signoria.com

Castello del Trebbio

When touring around Florence, gawping at the city's architectural splendours and being surrounded by tourists from all over the world, it is easy to forget that you are in Tuscany – the Tuscany of endless, rolling hills dotted with typical Italian villas and penetrated by slim country roads. The good news is that the quintessential Tuscany experience many dream about is only a 30 minute drive away from the city, and can be had at Castello del Trebbio, a 12th century castle which housed both the Pazzi and Medici families, and now offers an unforgettable experience in the heart of the fairy tale Tuscan countryside.

Originallybuilt as a fortress in the twelfth century for the Pazzi family, the castles proprietary was taken over by the Medici family who proceeded to turn the fortress into a luxury villa.

Today, the castle is surrounded by olive groves – with over 10,000 olive trees - and grape vines and has been fully restored to its original state, with the current owners having respected its long history.

Tourists either visit for the day to explore the wine cellars, and to sample the top quality olive oil along with the cheese and meat platters the castle offers. Wine tours are also very common; however most visits are by tourists looking to spend time relaxing in Tuscan countryside in one of the castles apartments or villas. There is also pasta making classes, a fantastic restaurant and outdoor swimming pool.

Via Santa Brigida, 9
50060 Santa Brigida (Florence)
Italy
(+39) 055 830 4900
http://www.vinoturismo.it/

Price for stays less than seven days: €50 per person per night, with reduced prices for children under 12 years of age. There is a minimum stay of two nights. Apartments need to be booked for at least one week.

The Medici Villas

Said to be the godfathers of the Renaissance, the Medici were a powerful family who rose from a small Italian community to amass unparalleled wealth, spearhead the Renaissance, and rule Europe for over 300 years. With a huge interest in education, they pushed for a rebirth in all forms, and were not afraid to spend in order to encourage a new world approach to learning.
This resulted in a lot of investment from the family in the cities artistic heritage, which to this day has resulted in Florence being regarded as one of the world's most beautiful.

The Medici family owned numerous rural building complexes around the outskirts of Florence, which they used for recreation and holidays. Although all contrasting, the villas are known for their pristine gardens, classic architecture and interiors littered with artistic masterpieces from paintings and sculptures to antique furniture and adorning frescos.

The Medici Villa in Poggio a Caiano is straight forward to reach by public transport, while Florence Tour offer guided tours of a selection of the villas. See www.florencetour.com for more information.

The Medici Villa
Piazza de Medici 14,
59016 Poggio a Caiano
Tel.: (+39) 055 238 8796

Admission to the villa is free year round.
Opening hours: 8:15am until 6:30pm, with closing times depending on the season

A local bus service can take tourists to the gates of the villa, which depart from Via Nazionale near the train station. Take a bus leaving for either Poggio a Caiano, Pistoia or Quarrata, all three will stop directly in front of the villa.

Piazzale Michelangelo

A popular spot for a relaxing afternoon, Piazzale Michelangelo offers some of the best panoramic views of the city and its surrounding valley, and is a popular sunset spot for locals and tourists alike. The Piazza was designed in 1869 by local architect Giuseppe Poggi. He wanted to create a monument base for where Michelangelo's work could be displayed to the public.

While Poggi's vision was never realized – the intended building that was built to be the museum is now a restaurant – the piazza has become a major tourist spot in modern day Florence, primarily for its views. The piazza is filled with tourists and vendors, as well as a bronze replica of Michelangelo's David. The piazza can easily be reached by taking the number 12 or 13 bus from the center, while the double decker sightseeing buses also stop at the piazza. For the more adventurous, climbing up from Piazza Poggi – which sits at the base of the hill - will lead you to Piazzale Michelangelo.

It is important to remember that while most of the piazza is now a car park, there are limited things to do once at the top of the hill. The view alone is the prime reason many people like to spend an afternoon relaxing here.

Piazzale Michelangelo
50125 Firenze,
Italy
Tel.: (+39) 055 055

Boboli Garden & Pitti Palace

The Boboli Garden and its surrounding areas were created by the Medici in 1549 when Eleonora di Toledo - the wife of Duke Cosimo I - purchased the Palazzo Pitti. Cosimo I recruited the most renowned landscape gardeners of his time to lay out the expansive garden as a backdrop to their new palace where they resided. The garden also hosts to a fantastic collection of statues and fountains.

Over the years the garden was expanded many times as more and more statues and fountains were added, before the garden was opened to the public in 1776. From the top of the terraces you can find remarkable vistas of Florence and the surrounding Arno Valley. There is an amphitheater within the Boboli Garden situated just behind the Pitti Palace, and this and was once the location of the quarry that gave the palace its stone.

Palazzo Pitti,
Piazza dèPitti, 1,
50125 Firenze,
Italy
Tel.: (+39) 055 229 8732
Web: www.giardinodiboboli.it

Hours: Daily, 8:15am until 4:30pm (November February); 8:15am until 5:30pm (March); 8:15am until 6:30pm (April, May, September and October; 8:15am until 5:30pm (October when Daylight Saving Time ends); 8:15am until 7:30pm (June and August). Entry is permitted up to an hour before closing time.

Cost: Adults and all non-EU, €7; EU citizens aged 18 to 25, €3.50; EU citizens aged below 18 or older than 65, FREE. ID is required for EU citizens.

Basilica di San Miniato al Monte

Just a five minute walk from the Piazzale Michelangelo is the San Miniato al Monte church – meaning St. Minias on the Hill - one of Tuscany's most original and bona fide Romanesque churches. Designed by Giuseppe Poggi, the church is surrounded by a series of stairs and terraces, and built between 1865 and 1873. Like the aforementioned surrounding places, the area also offers a spectacular view of the city and is usually explored in conjunction with the Piazzale Michelangelo.

The church has its own interesting history, and was built above the grave of Saint Minias. He was decapitated and buried at the top of the hill, with the church being built shortly after he was buried. The façade was created in 1090, and has an elegant, green and white marble coloured decoration. The basilica also houses a partially finished campanile, which was created in 1523, replacing an older tower that had collapsed in 1499. The current bell tower was used to defend the city during the siege of Florence in 1529 and 1530, by the then ousted Medici and their followers.

Via Monte alle Croci,
Firenze,
Italy.
(+39) 055 234 2731
www.san-miniato-al-monte.com

Recommendations for the Budget Traveller

Places to Stay

While Florence has never, and probably will never be regarded as a cheap getaway, there are certainly options dotted all around the city for inexpensive places to stay and eat, by western European standards. The best rates for hostels and Bed and Breakfasts can be found between September and April, while most hotels have special offers on outside of the summer season.

Accommodations and restaurants with the lowest prices are typically located a little outside of the tourist meccas of Plaza del Signoria and other notable points of interest in the city centre, and sometimes just a ten or fifteen minute walk away from the main squares and attractions can yield more reasonable prices for the budget traveller.

Hotel Sampaoli

Via San Gallo, 14
50129 Firenze,
Italy
Tel.: (+39) 055 284 834
Web: http://www.hotelsampaoli.it/

Rates: €29-€32.50 per person per night for a private double or twin room with a shared bathroom (+€5 per person per night for en-suite bathroom.) The hotel also offers private three bed (€27), four bed (€23), and five bed (€19) rooms, all with private en-suite bathrooms, and all prices quoted per person per night.

Situated within a 1000 year old building, and in the heart of Florence, the Hotel Sampaoli offers guests a quiet and simple stay, while being just minutes away from the all of the major attraction and transportation hubs offered by the city. The Santa Maria Novella train station, which connects Florence the rest of Italy, is just minutes away, while a short walk in the opposite direction will lead you to the Duomo and the Accademia Gallery.

All rooms offer a TV with DCD player, and all have access to the hotels free Wi-Fi, and the welcoming atmosphere provided by the staff will help ensure a pleasant stay in the city of art.

Garibaldi's Relais & Charme

Via Pratese 34,
Florence,
Italy
Tel.: (+39) 055 342 4625
Web: http://relaisgaribaldis.wordpress.com/

Rates: €12-€14 for a mixed or female only dorm; €38.50 per person per night in a private twin or double room.

Located just ten minutes away from the city centre in a peaceful, residential area of Florence, Garibaldi Relais is a family run villa set within the lush greenery of its own private garden, and offers both business and leisure travelers a relaxing retreat away from the hustle and bustle of the city centre. The guest rooms are decorated in a classic style, with Wi-Fi access, tea and coffee making facilities, and fresh linens, while the villa also has a computer station located in the lobby.

Additionally facilities include the offer of free parking, bicycle hire, an on-site café, an outdoor terrace and free city maps. GarbaldiRelais is located just minutes away from the main railway station, the business district and the Roberto Cavalli shopping outlet for those looking for some retail therapy.

Hostel Greci

Borgodei Greci 13, Florence, Italy
Tel:(+39) 349 360 0709
Web: http://www.hostelgreci.hostel.com/

Rates: €59 per person per night for a double or twin room with a private en-suite bathroom. €49 for a female only, two bed dorm.

For those wanting to be in the heart of the action at the best possible price, the Hostel Greci is located in the heart Florence, and is a short walk from all of the city centre's major attractions, being just one minute from the Uffizi, Plaza dellaSignoria and the Ponte Vecchio.

The hostel offers a warm ambience, with a common room, 24 hour security, tours desk and luggage storage, while all rooms come with fresh linens and a reading light.

David Inn

Via Ricasoli 31
Firenze, Italy
Tel: (+39) 055 213 707
Web: http://www.davidinn.hostel.com/

Rates: €25-€27 per person per night in a four bed mixed dorm.

Another property in the heart of Florence, the David Inn is located just one block away from its namesake and most famous David in the city, Michelangelo's David, housed inside the Accedemia Gallery. The hostel also has views of the nearby Duomo. The hostel has gained a reputation for its cleanliness, and its bright, airy, and quiet rooms.

Major facilities include a common room, free internet access, luggage storage, personal lockers, free city maps from the tours desk and cable TV, while all rooms come equipped with individual reading lights, hot showers, and linens.

Soggiorno Pitti

Palazzo Pitti, 8
50125 Firenze,
Italy
Tel.: (+39) 055 392 1483
Web: www.soggiornopitti.com

Rates: €33-€38 for a single room, €23.50 per person per night for a twin or double (shared bathroom) and €30 for a twin or double with a private en-suite bathroom.

The mixed dorm is €16 per person per night, while the hostel also offers private three bed (€25) and four bed (€22) rooms both with a private en-suite bathroom.

Housed in an early twentieth-century building on the north side of the Arno River, and within the historic center of Florence, the SoggiornoPitti is situated just in front of Pitti Palace and offers convenient access to the nearby sites or to the Ponte Vecchio where you can cross and be in the Plaza dellaSignoria within minutes.

Facilities include a large, free breakfast, common room, internet access, café, luggage storage and tours desk.

Places to Eat

Florence as a whole is consistently held in the upper echelons of city's which have a remarkable and outstanding food options, and this catering isn't just reserved for the fancy, overpriced restaurants aimed at free spending tourists. There are a plethora of options available ranging from sit down restaurants, hole-in-the-wall eateries and a wealth of quick fix dessert options for those with a sweet tooth.

Le Campane

Borgo La Croce 85/87.
50124 Firenze, Italy
Tel.: (+39) 55-23-41-101
Web: www.le-campane.it

Price: between €8 and €11 per person for dinner.

After undergoing a major facelift in 2006, Le Campane is a classic Italian Pizzeria, and offers two air conditioned rooms with great wall art and images for those wanting to dine in, while also offering a reasonable take out menu for those wanting to take some fresh pizza back to their lodgings. There is also an outside dining area.

The restaurant offers a full lunch and dinner menu at rock bottom prices in comparison to many city centre restaurants in Florence, although it is best known for its pizzas. The Margherita and Neopolitan pizzas are very well received, and both highly recommended.

IL GIOVA

Via Borgo
La Croce, 73
Firenze, Italy
Tel.: (+39) 055 248 0639
Web: www.ilgiova.com
Price: From €11 per person.

Possibly one of the smallest restaurants in the city, this is a great family run restaurant offering freshly made bread, pasta and sauces, and excellent service to boot. Located a little walk from the centre of Florence, on the east side in the La Croce area, Il Giova is slowly becoming one of the city's worst kept secrets, and reservations are recommended for dinner.

Highly recommended is the filet mignon, or the pork fillet with caramelized onions, while the chocolate cake for dessert has earned rave reviews.

Il Pizza Iuolo

Via dèMacci, 113
50122 Firenze,
Italy
Tel.: (+39) 055 241 171
Web: www.ilpizzaiuolo.it

Price: €8-€22 per person for dinner.

A bustling restaurant located in the centre of Florence, IlPizzaiuolo offers some of the best appetizers in the city, with the house appetizer changing regularly. Neopolitan thick crust pizza is a highlight from the pizza menu, while the spaghetti al vongole is well received from the mains menu. The restaurant is extremely popular amongst both local Florentine's and tourists alike, and this shows in the warm, bubbly atmosphere that hits you when you walk into the place. Because of its popularity, reservations are highly recommended to avoid the long wait time, or going outside of the prime time hours (7:30pm to 9:30pm).

Grom

Via delle Oche,
50122 Firenze,
Italy
Tel.: (+39) 055 216 158
Web:www.grom.it
Price: €3-€6

With stores throughout Italy, Grom is held in high regard for its Gelato, which come in many different choices and included a variety of chocolates. Although it can be tricky to find - situated down a narrow side street - there is normally a line up at the store, paying testament to wealth of positive reviews and hype this gelateria has gained. Being just metres away from the Duomo, Grom is a perfect pit stop for the inevitable, late night Italian Gelato experience.

Blue River

Lungarno Delle Grazie 12,
Florence, Italy
Price: €7.50 meals. Desserts: From €3

A small hole-in-the-wall restaurant located between the Uffizi and the Bibliotecha, the Blue River offers a drink, a large salad and main course for just €7.50, and is an ideal choice for tourists on a budget. The restaurant is also popular with local Florentine's who chat to the owner over home pressed coffee while he tends to the line of customers.

With some fantastic desserts and sweets also available, the Blue River is perfect for grabbing a filling lunch or just a quick stop-gap.

Places to Shop

Whether you are in the market for some leather goods, gold, or just some good old retail therapy, Florence, like all major Italian cities can offer some of the world's biggest names.

While the top end designers like Gucci, Ferragamo, Pucci, and Armani are all located around the streets of the streets of Via Tornabuoni, Via dellaVignaNuova, and Via deiCalzaiuol, there are also options that won't break the bank, and will ensure some memorabilia from your Florence trip.

Stockhouse Il Giglio

Borgo Ognissanti 64
50123 Firenze

For those interested in the fashion labels, but not too keen on the price nor the season, pay a visit to the Stockhouse Giglio sells 'last year's trends' – a big no-no for fashion followers, yet hardly a problem for the majority of shoppers - at a fraction of their original prices, due to the inability to shift these in the original stores. While some clothes can hold their prices, it is definitely worth a visit as both men and women's designer clothing can be found for a great bargain.

Farmacia del Mercato Centrale

Via dell'Ariento, 87-r
50123 Firenze

A must for food fanatics, the Farmacia del Mercato Centrale offers some of the freshest produce in the city at reasonably low prices. Known for its fantastic choice of great meat, bread and cheese, the store is also popular – and highly recommended – for those staying in Florence longer than a few days and who would like to pick up some local produce to cook at their apartment.

Trade here has been in operation for over 100 years, with some of the original signage and jars still on display.

Monaco Metropolitano

Via Ramaglianti, 6/R
50125 Firenze
Tel.: (+39) 055 268 121
Web: www.monacometropolitano.com
Email: monacometropolitano@gmail.co

For those in the hunt for leather, all offerings might seem the same when browsing the many outlets in Florence. This is where Monaco Metropolitano is different. Located on the north side of the Arno River, in the district known as Oltarno, it is just a few minutes' walk from the Ponte Vecchio, and offers a remarkable collection of handmade leather products, which are created daily by the skilled staff using original methods and tools combined with modern ideas.

New ideas and designs are born every day, and one can watch the skilled old timers or enthusiastic students show you the process of making such products by hand.

Pisa

Pisa is best known for the world famous Leaning Tower of Pisa but it offers much more. In addition to its magnificent buildings and ancient monuments, Pisa provides some of the most beautiful views in all of Tuscany and is just a short drive away from the scenic hill towns and villages of Tuscany including Siena and Lucca.

Pisa was a bustling port in the 10th and 11th centuries. In 1944 during the Second World War, Pisa was attacked for 45 days. Thousands of its inhabitants were killed and half of the city's buildings were destroyed. Despite this the architecture, art and sculpture of the city are still its biggest attractions.

Pisa has retained so much of its historical look and feel that UNESCO has named it a World Heritage site.

Because the city center is quite small the best way to enjoy the sights is to walk the streets of the old city. Some of the most famous examples of architectural treasures in Pisa can be found in the Piazza deiMiracoli or Square of Miracles. This is a very large square with an immaculately tended lawn that has been there since the 11th century and which lies next to medieval walls that are still standing in the heart of the old city. The four marble buildings that rise out of that lawn combine the architecture of the Moors along with Celtic and Roman architecture and are some of Italy's most famous landmarks. The buildings include the cathedral known as the Duomo di Pisa, the world famous Leaning Tower of Pisa which was built as a bell tower for the cathedral, the Baptistery and the Monumental churchyard or Camposanto.

Throngs of travelers come to see these architectural marvels every year making Pisa one of the most important tourist sites in Italy. But that is not all that Pisa has to offer. The city also boasts several museums which are worth visiting for the architecture of the buildings themselves as well as the art and sculpture on display inside. Pisa's museums contain the works of many of the great Italian artists and are a must see for anyone with an appreciation of beauty and form.

The great physicist and astronomer Galileo Galilei was born in Pisa and his birthplace is still clearly marked and the city's international airport is named after him. Galileo attended the university in Pisa and studied for a medical degree before becoming a scientist. According to local folklore Galileo is said to have dropped objects from the tower of Pisa in an effort to see if heavier objects fell faster than smaller ones of the same material. There is no evidence to prove that this really happened but it is a great story to tell just the same.

Like pretty much anywhere else in Italy the food in Pisa is a gourmand's delight. Because it lies on the coast, Pisa is well known for its seafood dishes such as 'Bavettine Sui Pesce' which is flattened spaghetti seasoned with a delicious white sauce, mussels soup which is served on Tuscan bread and Frog soup. If seafood is not your favorite, however, the city also offers delectable land dishes and of course desserts, a favorite of which is the 'tortacoivischeri' which is a cake made with pine-seeds, raisins, chocolate and citrus candy. There is also a variety of local wines to accompany all the wonderful food.

Culture

Pisa is a university town with the University of Pisa students numbering 60,000 in a city that only 100,000 people call home. The university is one of Italy's oldest. It was established in 1343 and is considered one of country's best. Pisa is also home to the Scuola Normale Superiore an educational institute which has its origins in Paris and which has been around since 1810. Only the best students were admitted to this institute and it is still considered an elite school.

The city of Pisa has the vibe that all university towns have where you feel that a party can get started anywhere at any time and the students do often organize parties and other music events that are open to the public. There are of course nightclubs in Pisa as well as several pubs and pizza parlors such as the Millie Bar that boasts a vibrant Karaoke night every Tuesday because everyone knows that Italians love to sing. Many visitors enjoy just walking around the city center at night alongside the low walls around the river. Because it is a university city there are also always low priced accommodations available for the budget traveler.

Location & Orientation

Pisa is a city in the region of Tuscany, in Central Italy in the province of Pisa, close to Lucca and Florence. It is one of the chief towns in that region. It is located on the bank of the mouth of the River Arno on the Tyrrhenian Sea.

Climate & When to Visit

Pisa has warm, sunny summers as is common in the Mediterranean with the peak summer months of June to August being quiet hot and Pisa experiences temperatures of 30 degrees Centigrade regularly. In the wintertime it is cooler and quite wet and fog is a possibility. Although it doesn't really get very cold it can get windy so warm clothes are needed if you are going to visit between November and February.

If you are lucky enough to be in Pisa on the 16th of June you will witness the Luminara festival or Fiesta di san Ranieri. This festival is held to celebrate the city's patron saints day. In the evening of that day all the lights along the river go out or are lowered and 10,000 candles or torches are lit. There are also street events and fireworks displays. The city's monuments look even more beautiful by candlelight and this festival should not be missed.

One of the city's largest events is the Giocodel Ponte or Game of the Bridge which also takes place in the month of June and which has been around since the 16th century. The Game involves a series of challenges among twelve teams made up of people from the north and south banks of the city. They dress in medieval costumes.

Sightseeing Highlights

Piazza dei Miracoli (Square of Miracles)

56010 Pisa, Italy

The Piazza del Miracoli or Square of Miracles is a walled square located in central Pisa which dates back to the pre-Roman era. It is famous for the architecture of the building that can be found there as well as its cultural heritage and has been named by UNESCO as a World Heritage Site.

It was given its name by the Italian poet Gabriele D'Annunzio who described the square that way in one of his books and is not to be confused with the Campo deiMiracoli in the fictional story of Pinnocchio.

The large square is also sometimes called the Piazza del Duomo after one of the buildings there. Made mostly of grass but with some paved areas, the Piazza is best known for the 4 marble buildings which stand in it and which are some of the most famous buildings in the world. All built between the 11th and 14th century, the four religious structures are the Duomo or Cathedral, the Campanile or bell tower, the Battistero or Baptistery and the Composanto or walled cemetery.

Apart from the four famous structures the square is also home to the OspedaleNuovo di Santo Spirito which was built as a hospital in the 13th century by Italian architect Giovanni di Simone. Its name translates to the new Hospital of the Holy Spirit but it is now home to the museum of Sinopias which you can visit to view the original drawings of the walled cemetery which is also located in the field. The hospital is made of red brick unlike the other buildings in the square which are white marble and it was restructured in 1562.

The Square of Miracles is considered to be one of the best places in the world for viewing and appreciating medieval art. Everyone who visits Pisa spends some time there and it is very easy to reach from either the airport or the train station.

Leaning Tower of Pisa

Piazza Arcivescovado, 6, Pisa

The Leaning Tower of Pisa is also called Le Torre Pisa or la Campanile (a bell tower that is free-standing).

It was built as the bell tower of the city's cathedral and the objective was to demonstrate the wealth of the city at the time. It is now considered one of the seven wonders of the Medieval World. When work began on the Tower in August of 1173, its design and the way it was being constructed was ahead of its time.

The intention was that the Tower would be vertical but after the 3rd floor was built it began to lean. The reason was not known at the time but it has since been discovered that the Tower was built on a clay mixture which was too soft to support the construction without sinking and the foundation was only 3 meters deep so the building began to lean in a southwesterly direction. Despite this, or perhaps because of it, the tower is considered the world over to be a great work of art and many people visit Pisa just to see it.

When the lean was first noticed in 1178, work on the Tower stopped. It began again in 1272 under the direction of Giovanni did Simone but stopped again in 1284 because of the battle of Meloria against the people of Genoa, Pisa's enemies at that time. The Pisans lost that battle.

The design of the Tower would be worth seeing even if it did not lean. The exterior is made of white marble and under the marble is limestone and lime mortar and it is that material that is most likely responsible for the fact that the building is still standing. The tower of Pisa rises 55 meters into the air and has 8 stories. The stories are made up of marble columns stacked on top of each other. There are over 200 Corinthian columns in all. The floors at the top of the tower were built out from the vertical in the direction opposite to where the tower leans in an effort to serve as a counter balance.

On the bottom story of the tower there are 15 marble arches. The tower weighs over 14 hundred tons, has 207 columns, 30 arches on each level above the ground floor and is said to be listing by about 10%. The inside walls of the cylindrical tower as well as the outer walls are made of limestone and it is hollow inside. There's a spiral staircase that is also made of marble and which is made up of 294 steps. The stairway goes up to the sixth level and in the actual bell chamber there are seven bells which are all properly tuned. The bells are housed in cells like windows. The bell chamber was completed in 1372 and work on the tower stopped after that until the 1800s.

When the bell tower was built 7 bells were put in. Each bell had a name. They were called L'Assunta, Il Crocifisso, San Ranieri, La Pasquereccia, Del Pozzetto, La Terza and Il Vespruccio. La Pasquereccia is the oldest bell. It was cast in 1262 by Lotteringo and carries an inscription that indicates when it was made and by whom. It also says that the bell was paid for by someone called Gerardo Hospilatarius.

The engravings on the bell include drawings of animals, angels and other religious depictions. Before it was put in the Tower the Pasquereccia was the bell used in the Tower of Justice to announce when criminals were being executed. It was most likely rung when Count Ugolino died. The bell weighs over 2000 lbs. and is also called La Giustiza. The largest bell is L'Assunta, named after Our Lady of the Assumption, which is made of gold and was cast in 1654 by Giovanni Pietro. It weighs nearly 8,000 lbs and carries an inscription that says "The angels raise the Virgin Mary to heaven and rejoicing and praising, they bless Our Lord."

The bells were rung using a bell cord from the ground but there was concerned that the swinging could affect the Tower so that was stopped. It was replaced by clappers within the bells that are activated by electromagnets.

Several people have worked on the tower but no one knows architect designed it. It was finished by Tommaso Pisano who built the belfry. In 1838 an architect named Alessandro Della Gherardesca decided to put in a pathway at the base of the Tower so that visitors could see the intricate work done on the base of the Tower. This made the building lean more.

FLORENCE & PISA TRAVEL GUIDE

In 1964 the Italian government led by Benito Mussolini, embarrassed by the continued leaning of the building asked for help and a team of professionals came together and decided to put in an 800 ton counter weight. They did this by drilling into the foundation and pouring in cement. Unfortunately the cement sank into the clay soil under the square and made things worse. The tower was closed to the public in 1990 in case the crowds make the leaning worse and it remained closed to visitors until 2001. The bells were removed and the building was anchored during that time. The engineers who worked on the Tower at that time believe that the building will remain at the angle it was then for several hundred years unless there is a major earthquake. It is currently open and a very popular site.

If you plan to visit the Tower it is a good idea to book your ticket online or in person a couple of weeks in advance so that you can avoid the long lines and that way you can also ensure that the tickets don't sell out before you get yours. People who book in advance also go straight to the top of the line. Advance tickets to climb the tower cost 17 Euros which is 2 Euros more than if you buy your ticket at the box office but you will definitely be able to climb the tower that day.

Twice every hour people are allowed in and if you buy an advanced ticket you will be allocated a certain time to enter. You have to ensure that you are there at the time. It takes about 10 minutes to climb the stairs and many people have reported feeling dizzy because of the tilt of the building. The Tower is opened from 10 in the morning to 5 in the afternoon from November to February except for Christmas day and January 7 when the tower opens from 9 am to 6pm. From March 21 to June 15 the hours are 8:30 am to 8:30 pm. For the rest of June and until August 31 the tower is open to the public from 8:30 am to 11 pm. All through September you can visit the Tower from 8:30 am to 8:30 pm while the schedule for October is 9:00 am to 7:00 pm.

Bell Tower of San Nicola Church

Via Santa Maria
56100, Pisa, Italy

Known by locals as Campanile di San Nicola, the bell tower at San Nicola church is sometimes overlooked because of the popularity of the city's other bell tower, the Leaning Tower of Pisa, but it is certainly worth seeing. Built in the Pisan-Romanesque style of architecture, the eight-sided tower is also found in central Pisa and is actually also leaning a bit. The base is already below the level of the road.

No one is quite sure when the tower was built but researchers believe it was built in 1170 and that Diotisalvi was the architect. Different types of stones, such as limestone, Elba granite and Apuan marble were brought in from different locations to give the tower its multicolored look. The marble was used to construct the columns.

Inside the tower is a spiral staircase which researchers recently discovered was designed based on the geometric studies done by Pisan mathematician Leonardo Fibonacci. The stairway has a wall on the external side only. The tower also has a roof that is shaped like a pyramid.

The bell-chamber of the tower has six sides and each side has a window. There is only one bell in the chamber. At present the public is not allowed inside the tower but the outside alone is worth the visit.

Duomo di Pisa (Cathedral of Pisa)

Piazza dei Miracoli
56010 Pisa, Italy

The Cathedral was the first building that was erected in the Square of Miracles. Construction began in 1064. The Catholic Cathedral is an example of Romanesque architecture although there are traces of other styles to be found on the building including the influence of the Arabs with whom Pisa had many battles. It was the spoils of some of these battles that were used to finance the construction of the cathedral. The Cathedral is one of the largest in the world and is nearly 600 years old. It is 30 stories high and has 464 steps which the public is allowed to climb. The outside walls are much more ornate than the inside.

The main architect of the structure was Buschelo and he is buried in the Cathedral. After him in the 12th century came the architect Rainaldo who built the white marble façade of the Cathedral. The stones on the exterior of the structure are engraved with ancient inscriptions. The Cathedral is sometimes referred to as the Primatial because the Archbishop of Pisa has been a primate since the year 1672.

In 1595 there was a fire in the cathedral that destroyed most of the medieval art that was displayed there. Luckily they were replaced by equally if not more beautiful works from the Renaissance era. Some of the original works survived the fire so there are also some medieval pieces such as the bronze door called the door of San Ranieri which was made in 1180 by Bonnano Pisano and which features scenes from the bible. The tomb of Emperor Henry VII which was done by Tino di Camaino in 1315 can be found in the cathedral as well as the bones of Pisa's patron saint Saint Ranieri. The Cathedral was consecrated in 1118 by Pope Gelasius II. Pope Gregory VIII was also buried in the cathedral but the tomb was destroyed by the fire of 1595.

There are many other works of art inside the Cathedral that are worth seeing such as an ornate pulpit by the Italian sculptor and painter Giovanni Pisano that depicts biblical scenes which is one of the Cathedral's biggest attractions and a crucifix by the sculptor Giambologna. The inside walls are made of black and white marble and there is a dome adorned with frescoes and a ceiling of gold which carries the coat of arms of the house of Medici. There is also a mosaic fresco on the wall above the main altar done by the great Florentine painter Cimabue with the help of his students. The Cathedral is also slightly tiled although unlike the Bell Tower it is hardly noticeable. All these pieces and more combine to make the cathedral or Duomo one of the premier edifices to visit in Tuscany.

Battistero (Baptistery)

Piazza dei Miracoli, 56126 Pisa, Italy

The official name of this structure which is also found in the square of Miracles is the St. John Baptistery and it is where baptisms were performed. The structure is the largest baptistery in Italy and is dedicated to St. John the Baptist. The Baptistery is taller than the leaning Tower of Pisa if the statue of John the Baptist at the top is included. The design is Roman but there is also evidence of Islamic influences and this is because construction on the baptistery started soon after the crusades. The Baptistery is made of marble.

Work began on this structure, which is nearly as big as the cathedral, in the year 1152 and was led by Diotisalvi. We know this because his name is carved on one of the interior pillars. Work stopped sometime after and a hundred years passed before work was again started on the baptistery because of a lack of funds. Construction was continued by Giovanni and Nicola Pisano and it was never finished until 1363. Because it took so long to complete, the baptistery has a mix of architectural styles with the lower portion being Romanesque and the upper section Gothic. The upper part of the building has the pointed arches associated with Gothic architecture while the lower portion has rounded gothic arches.

There are even two domes with roofs that are half lead, half tiles. The Baptistery is a circular building several floors high with a carved marble exterior and columns right around. Diotisalvi did not have that shape in mind when he began construction but when he died his successor Nicola Pisano changed the plans to a more Gothic style and it is he who added an external roof over the internal pyramid roof. The shape was supposed to resemble that of the Holy Sepulcher. Inside the Baptistery there are 8 tall columns and 4 pillars which form the central area. The roof is made up of a double dome which has a very unusual shape and which was added at the end of construction in the 14th century. The outer walls are very ornate while the interior has little decoration.

One of the main attractions of the Baptistery is a pulpit which the sculptor Nicola Pisano carved which can be found in the central area of the structure. The pulpit has six sides and on it there are scenes from the bible and other scenes such as one of a naked Hercules. It was created between 1255 and1260. On one corner of the sculptor there is a carving of Daniel that supports that side. There is also an eight sided baptismal font which was created by Guido Bigarellie da Como in 1246. It is next to the pulpit which is another big attraction along with a bronze sculpture by ItaloGriselli.

The artwork on the walls of the Baptistery depicts the life of john the Baptist and on the upper floors there is a depiction of Jesus Christ flanked by John the Baptist and the Virgin Mary with angels all around. A spiral staircase which takes you up the women's gallery and another staircase takes you right into the dome.

The acoustics of the building is one of the most fascinating aspects of the Battistero. It came about because of the double roof and every half hour or so a choir sings so that the sound can be appreciated. If you can sing feel free to try it out. Like most of the buildings in the Square of Miracles the baptistery leans slightly.

Camposanto (Walled Cemetery)

Piazza dei Miracoli, 56126 Pisa

Founded in 1277 the cemetery was intended as a place for the stone and marble tombs called sarcophagi in which local aristocrats were buried and that were scattered all over the nearby cathedral. It was completed in 1464.the legend states that the soil of the cemetery was brought to Pisa at the end of the Crusades by Ubaldo de Lanfranch. It is thought to be holy soil taken from Golgotha, the place where Jesus Christ was crucified.

The cemetery has 43 arches and 2 magnificent bronze doors by Ghiberti which are some of the main attractions. One doorway has a Gothic Tabernacle which depicts the Virgin Mary with child and 4 saints. The doorways that you would see if you visited the baptistery are replicas as the originals are in the Museo dell'Opera del Duomo in order to conserve them. The building also contains many statues and carvings of gothic design and sculptures

In the 14th century beautiful frescos were added to the inside of the walls. They were on the then controversial themes of Life and Death and were created by two artists who were very popular at the time, Francesco Traini and Bonamico Buffalmacco. These were later added to by other Italian artists who added stories of the saints and the Old Testament.

In the 16th century the tombs of members of the ruling Medici family and esteemed local university lecturers were also placed in the cemetery. It was later utilized as a museum.

During World War II, the Camposanto was badly damaged by a bomb dropped by the Allied forces in 1944. The bomb destroyed many priceless artifacts and efforts have been made to restore the building to its former glory and they have largely been successful.

Museo dell'Opera del Duomo

Piazza dell'Arcivescovado 8, 56126 Pisa (PI)

The Museo dell'Opera del Duomo in English means the Museum of the Cathedral Works and this museum houses many of the works of art that were formerly kept in the city's cathedral or Duomo. The museum is located where the Episcopal seminary used to be in the square of Miracles.

The Museum was created to display all the medieval art which was previously scattered all over the structures in the square. The museum has about 200 paintings that date from the 12th to the 16th century. Among its exhibits are the sculptures that were created by the famous Italian sculptors Nicola Pisano and Giovanni Pisano. One of the highlights of a visit to this museum would be the ivory carving by Giovanni Pisano of the Madonna and child which he made for the altar. There are also marble decorations that look distinctly Moorish in design.

After the war other works of art were placed in the museum and it is now home to a collection of religious garments, manuscripts and other items from the cathedral, including models of the Duomo, which make up what is called the Cathedral collection. There are also some relics from Italy, and Egypt as well as some Etruscan relics that had been on display in other buildings in the Square of Miracles since the beginning of the 19th century.

One of the highlights of the display is a wooden crucifix form the 12th century and a bronze griffin that was brought back from the Crusades. Be sure to see the sketches of the frescoes of the Camposanto that were made during the restoration in the 19th century. The restorer created etchings and his son colored them in. The Museum has the prints of these etchings that show what the paintings in the Camposanto before the bombing during the war looked like.

The art is divided into rooms with the pieces related to the architecture of the Cathedral such as models and plans, being displayed in the first room. The Romanesque art such as the 12th century crucifix and the bronze griffin are in room 3, while room six houses the statues by Giovanno Pisano and other precious items such as a cross that was used to lead soldiers to battle during the first Crusade.

Perhaps one of the best the best reasons to visit the Museum other than the ancient artifacts is the great view that you get of the leaning tower next door from the second floor courtyard. The price of admission for the Museum is 5 Euros. The Museum is open from 9 am to 7:30 pm Monday to Saturday and on Sundays from 9 am to 1:45 pm.

Museo Nazionale di San Matteo

Piazza San Matteo in Soarta,
Lungarno Mediceo, 56100 Pisa

Translated into English the name of this museum is the National Museum of St. Matthew. This museum is in a building on the waterfront north of the river Arno in central Pisa. The structure dates back to the 11th century. It was once a Benedictine convent and the original paintings are still visible on the walls. The museum collects religious works and has about 200 paintings. Some of the paintings and decorations on the walls are from the middle Ages and they have a distinctively Islamic feel.

Displayed in the museum are paintings and sculptures from the 12th to the 15 century from some of Italy's most famous artists including Madonna of Humility by Fra Angelico and St Paul by Masaccio. The museum also has as part of its collection Pisan sculptures from churches in the area that have been moved to the museum to protect them from pollution including several painted crosses. One noteworthy sculpture is a statue of the Madonna from the 14th century that was created by Andrea Pisano who is from the area. Copies of the sculptures have been put into the churches to replace the originals.

This museum is one of the most important in Europe for medieval art. It also has an important collection of art from Tuscany. The art is divided into sections with the sculptures and the older paintings being in the first room. There is also a section for manuscripts which are all lit including a bible with illustrations from the 11th century. It is definitely a place worth visiting and for 5.00 Euros you will certainly get your money's worth.

The museum opens from 8:30 am to 7:00 pm most days except for Saturday and Sunday when it closes earlier at 1:00 pm and Mondays when it is closed.

Palazzo dell' Orologio

Piazza dei Cavalieri
56126 Pisa (PI), Italy

The name means Clock Palace or Tower and you can find it in the Piazza del Cavalieri.

Inside the building is the Library of the ScuolaNormaleSupiore but in the middle ages the Palazzo had a very different purpose.

The Clock Tower was designed by Vasari and is made up of two buildings that were connected by a vault in the early 1600s. It used to be a place where old or sick Knights of the St. Stefano knighthood were sent. The two buildings were called the Torre deiGualandi and the Mansion del Capitano. When they were joined they were then named the Palazzo del Buon Uomo or Palace of the Good Man. In 1696 the clock which was formerly housed in the steeple of the church of St. Stefano was moved there and put in the arc that joins the two buildings. As a result the building was renamed to its current title. The small bell tower was put on the top of the building in 1696.

The building on the left is called the Palazzo della Giustizia, which was a tower house and in which could be found the offices of the city's magistrates. On the other side was the tower itself which was called dei Gualandi or Torre del Muda. The latter name refers to the eagle which is the symbol of the city. The tower has a tragic story and is sometimes called Torre della Fame or Hunger Tower because a nobleman, Count Ugolino della Gherardesca along with his family was killed by starvation while imprisoned there for treason. Legend has it that the count became so hungry that he ate the body of his dead grandchild. The poet Dante used this story in his epic the Divine Comedy.

The side of the Palace is decorated with frescoes by the like of Giovanni Stefano Maruscelli, and Lorenzo Paladini among others.

Campanile di San Nicola (St. Nicolas Belfry)

Via Santa Maria
56100, Pisa, Italy

This is the second most famous bell tower in Pisa and it is located in the historical center of the city. St Nicolas Belfry was intended for the church which is next door. Its design is in the Pisan-Romanesque style and it was built in 1170 by Diotisalvi. The Belfry has eight sides and is made of limestone and Elba granite with Apuan marble for the columns. The bell tower is a hexagon in shape with a window on each side. There is only one bell in the tower. There is a staircase in the bell tower that is winding and that has a wall on the outer side only. It is said that this staircase was the inspiration for the one Renaissance architect Bramante put in the Vatican.

The tower is not open to the public but there is plenty to see from the outside.

Museum of the Ancient Ships

Medici Arsenale,
Ponte della Cittadella,
Pisa, Italy

These ships were found in 1998 when workers from the National Railway Company were digging in preparation for building an electrical station near the Pisa- San Rossore train station.

They found the remains of a harbor and what later turned out to be 16 wooden ships which were later found to date back to between 200 BC and 500 AD. Some of them were very well preserved and investigations have led them to believe that the ships are Roman. They are the only ships of this kind to be found in such good condition. Some of the ships still had cargo on them. Some of the items found were tall Roman jars, called amphorae containing preserved fruit such as plums and cherries as well as olives. One boat had a leather sandal and a wicker basket. Archeologists who were brought to the site also found stone, iron and wooden anchors as well as ropes and fishing equipment. The finds tell a lot about life in ancient Etruscan and Roman times as well as life in ancient Pisa.

Although the official Museum of the Ancient Ships is still being constructed there is an exhibition that is open to the public every day of the week. On weekends you can visit without reservations if you go between 10am and 12 noon or between 2:30 and 3:30 pm. During the week reservations must be made. It contains examples of all the artifacts found including the personal items of the sailors. A tour of the museum will also teach you about the floods that led to the submersion of the harbor and the ships.

Ussero Café

Lungarno Pacinotti 27
Palazzo dell' Ussero
56126 Pisa

The Caffedell'Ussero is a coffee house in a red brick structure called the Palazzo Agostini which is located on the right side of the river Arno. The cafe is in a Gothic building that was constructed in the 15th century. Café dell'Ussero was opened in 1775 and gets its name from the Italian word ussaro which refers to a soldier in the cavalry. It is one of the oldest cafes in Europe. The word is originally Hungarian and came to Italy via France.

The cafe once had a reputation for being the meeting place of Pisa's scholars from the nearby university. It was also a favorite of   the followers of the pro- politician Mazzini and some of the more liberal university lecturers. They gathered in the café to drink coffee, play billiards and discuss their political views. There is confirmation of these meetings in the town's police records from that time.

The café was turned into a cinema at the end of the 19th century. It was one of the first cinemas in the region. When the First World War ended Ussero was once again turned into a coffee house and the artists and literary types returned. Even today it is still a favorite haunt of the city's artists.

There are many stories of significant events that took place in this café and the walls carry testimony to many important and visitors. There are letters and other documents displayed that confirm the age and history of the establishment.

One of them the legends associated with the cafe is that in 1839 the Ussero café played host to meetings of the First Italian Congress of Scientists. The café has also seen other famous visitors such as the first director of the newspaper La Nazione, Alessandro D'Ancona and the Italian poet GuiseppiGiusti who talked of visiting the café in his memoirs. Other famous people who spent time at the Café include Charles Lindberg and the founder of the Futurist movement Gulieelmo Marconi. Many students from the local university spent time at the café and some of them have gone on to become Prime Ministers and Presidents and even receive the Noble Prize. There was even a collection of essays written about the coffee house called " L'Ussero: Un Caffe 'Universidario' nella Vita di Pisa". The café is open Monday to Friday 9am to 7pm.

Recommendations for the Budget Traveller

Places to Stay

Hotel Granduca Tuscany

Via San GiulianoTerme 13, 56017 , Pisa, Tuscany, Italy
Telephone: (+39) 050815029
www.hotelgranduca.it

This is a fairly new hotel which has parking, Internet access and a restaurant where a buffet breakfast is included at no extra charge.

The Hotel Granduca is next to a sporting center and guests are allowed to use the heated swimming pool and tennis courts. The hotel also has its own Wellness Center.

Hotel Granducca has 170 soundproof rooms and every guest has a television, a radio and a telephone. Some rooms have terraces. The hotel is conveniently located near to the main train station and it is also close to the thermal spa of San Giuliano. The price of a double room is $57 US per night.

Hotel Capitol

Via Enrico Fermi 13, 56126
Pisa, Tuscany, Italy
Telephone: (+39) 5049557
http://www.hotelcapitol.pisa.it

This hotel is located in the center of the city close to the University of Pisa in a historic old building but with very modern furnishing. It is ideally located in walking distance of the main visitor sights and is also close to shops and restaurants so you can leave your car in the parking lot and walk to wherever you want to go. For the animal lovers pets are allowed at this hotel.

Hotel Capitol has an internal courtyard as well as a lounge area and bar. The price of a double room is $97 US per night.

Hotel la Torre

Via Cesare Battisti 17, 56126,
Pisa, Tuscany, Italy
Telephone: (+39) 05025220

Hotel la Torre is in the city center near to the sights that are on every visitor's list including the Piazza deiMiracoli and the Pisa Royal Palace. It offers free wireless internet, and satellite TV. and phones in every room as well as multi-lingual staff and a free buffet breakfast.

A single room with a private bathroom is $80 US per night and a double is $94.

Hotel Francesco

Via Santa Maria, 129, 56126, Pisa, Italy
Telephone: (+39) 050 555453
http://www.hotlefrancesco.com

Hotel Francesco can be found in the center of Pisa in a very old building that has been renovated to house the hotel. It is close to all the famous historical sites and to the airport. In fact it is on the same street that leads to the Leaning Tower.

The hotel offers free internet and phone calls, a large terrace, and a restaurant that specializes in Tuscan dishes. The price of a double room is $128 US

Eden Park Tuscany Resort

Via Enrico Fermi 11, 56126,
Pisa, Tuscany, Italy
Telephone #: (+39) 050870252
http://www.edenparkpisa.it

Nestled in the Tuscan countryside near to the river, this resort is still close to the City center and the main sights. It is consists of 30 apartments each with 2 rooms which are in cottages and is surrounded by forest. There are several medieval villages nearby and a great view of the hills. Each cottage has its own kitchen and private access.

The resort offers nature tours, horseback riding, and paragliding. It is the perfect location for couples or families that want to get away from it all. The price of a single is $82 US while a double is $ 41 per person and a triple $36. Breakfast costs $10

Places to Eat & Drink

Il Montino

Vicolo del Moule 1,
Pisa, Italy

Il Montino is a pizzeria that offers the option of dining in or having take out.

There are only a few tables so get there early if you intend to eat in. the cost of a slice of pizza is Euro 1.50 while the average price of a meal is between $21 and $29. The pizzeria is open from 10:30 am to 3:00 pm then 5:00 pm to 10:00 pm Monday to Saturday.

Ristorante Turrido

Via D. Cavalca 64, Santa Maria,
Pisa, Italy

This indoor/outdoor restaurant is 20 minutes from the Leaning Tower and is known for its Tuscan dishes especially its pesto. The locals eat there and there is usually no better recommendation. This restaurant is also known to offer a wide array of desserts. It's open Monday to Saturday 6:30 pm to 10:30 pm

Peperosa Pisa

Via Renato Fucini N 10, 56126
Pisa, Italy
Telephone: (+39) 0503144170

The eatery offers Italian and Mediterranean fare and also has a wine bar. It is recommended that you make reservations. Prices for a meal range between $13 and $39 US and Peperisa is open Sunday through Saturday 11:00 am to 3:30 pm and 7:00 am to 12:00 midnight.

L'Ostellino

Piazza Felice Cavallotti 1
56126 Pisa

This diner is known for its sandwiches as it has a very wide assortment of fillings and fresh vegetables. Most of the sandwiches are available for between $4 and $8 and there are also meals available. L'Ostellino also has a bar so everything you need is in one place. The dress code for this diner is casual and no reservations are necessary. The restaurant does take out but not delivery and be sure to walk with cash or a debit card because credit cards are not accepted.

Coccio Bar & Gelateria

Via Santa Maria 86,
Pisa, Italy

This little restaurant specializes in local Italian cuisine and ice cream. It's near the leaning Tower and is known to offer a delicious breakfast. This eatery is known for its cappuccino as well as its salad. Coccio also serves sandwiches and other typical café food. Most of the fare at Coccio Bar can be had for under $10 US and the staff has a reputation for being very courteous and quick.

Places to Shop

Corso Italia

The Corso Italia is the High Street of Pisa with many shops and a lot to offer the shopper who does not want to spend a deal of money. It is usually a very busy and crowded street in the quarter of San Marino. On this street is a commercial center called the Corte di San Domenico. Further down the street near to the river a monthly antique market is held in a 17th century building called the Logge dei Banchi which used to be a jail.

The Corso Italia is also a good place to get a trendy haircut or buy a comic book for a specialty shop known as Fumettando. After working up an appetite from all the walking you can grab a slice of Pisan pizza or even buy a Nutella wafer.

Borgo Stretto

This street offers high-end shopping and boasts expensive shops and boutiques. Take a walk under the archways and watch the lovely window displays. When you need a break from shopping there are many cafes and ice cream parlors. Examples of shops to be found on this street are Valenti which has been in business since the 70s and which carries the latest in designer fashions for men and women and BB Maison. There are also stringed instrument shops that are a must for any visiting musician.

If you happen to be in Pisa at Christmas there is a market on Borgo Stretto where you can get some of the designer duds for less. There are also markets and shops on the side streets off of Borgo Stretto that offer better bargains.

Piazza dei Cavalieri & Ponti di Mezzo

There are open markets on these streets on the 2nd weekend of every month. These markets are a good place to find antiques at an affordable price. If you find something that appears to be too good a deal then it probably is so be very careful about what you purchase. It should be noted that the markets do not open in the months of July and August.

Piazza delle Vettovaglie

Scaliaureliosaffi
Livorno, 57123

This square is over one hundred years old and houses many shops as well as a fruit and food market. This is a good place to purchase wines and grocery items. It is also called the Central Market and is the largest indoor market in Europe. It is a covered market and is always very busy with people looking for fresh fruit and vegetables. Do not miss an opportunity to try the bread on sale especially the Tuscan 'saltless' bread or the star of the market the labronica or Pavilion fish which has been extremely popular for many years.

There are over 200 shops in the market as well as scores of wineries in the basement which can be accessed from two side doors and down the stairs. The market is also a wholesale market. There are also bars and cafes and it is open Monday to Friday from 7:00 am until 1:30 pm.

Via Buonarroti & Via San Martino

If you are looking for thrift shops and bargain shops then these two streets are the place to go. Via Buonarrotiis a busy market and both street markets open every Wednesday and Saturday. You can find clothes at these markets as well as fashion accessories and other items. Via Buonarroti offers many souvenirs and is one of the places where the locals shop.

FLORENCE & PISA TRAVEL GUIDE

Printed in Great Britain
by Amazon